Riding My Bike

T0020345

Staying Strong and Healthy

I can ride my bike.

3

I can ride my bike
to school.

I can ride my bike
to the beach.

I can ride my bike
to the track.

9

I can ride my bike
to the park.

I can ride my bike to the river.

I can ride my bike
to my friend's house.

I can ride my bike.